ANATOMY BOOK: Learn About Your Body Parts Edition

BODY PARTS

eyebrow
nose
ear
mouth
chest
arm
stomach
eye
forehead
hand
leg
knee
toe
foot

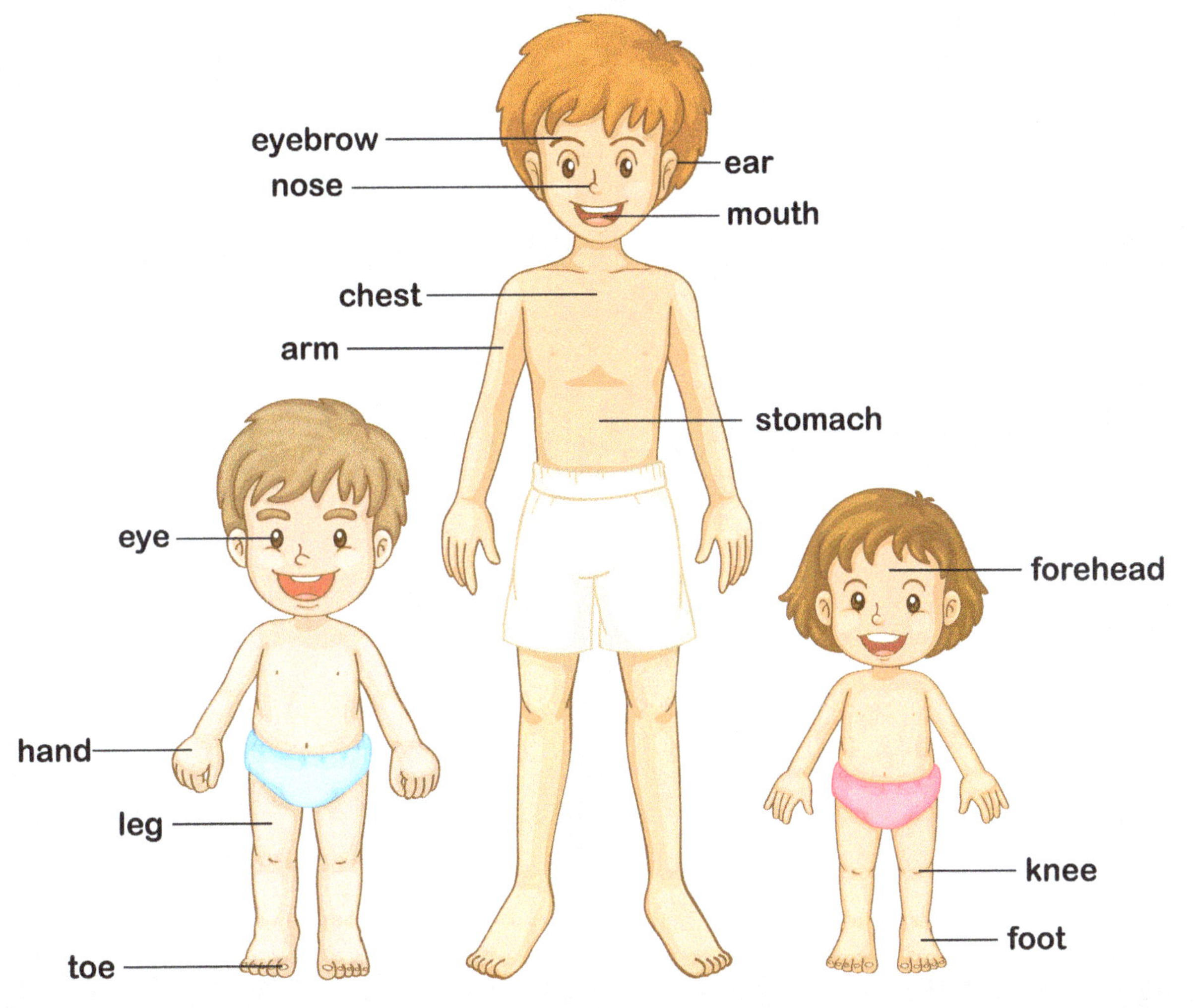

Abdomen/Stomach

The abdomen constitutes the part of the body between the chest and pelvis. The region enclosed by the abdomen is termed the abdominal cavity. Anatomically, the abdomen stretches from the thorax at the thoracic diaphragm to the pelvis at the pelvic brim.

Arm

The arm is made of three long bones, joined by a hinge joint at the elbow. The two bones of the lower arm are the radius and the ulna. The wrist is one of the best places to test our pulse. The upper arm bone is called the humerus or, jokingly, the funny bone.

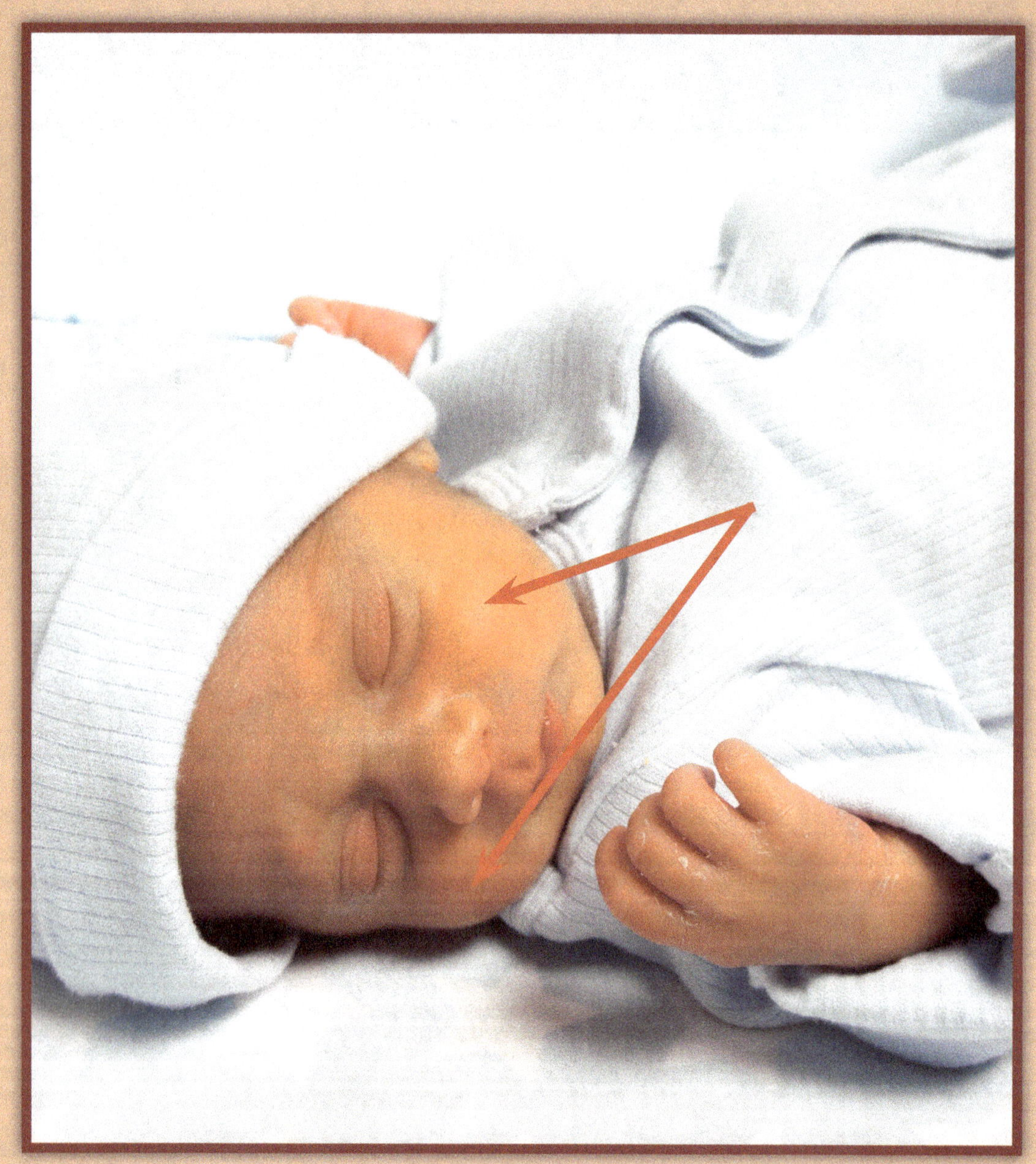

Cheek

Cheeks constitute the area of the face below the eyes and between the nose and the left or right ear. The area between the inside of the cheek and the teeth and gums is called the vestibule or buccal pouch or buccal cavity and forms part of the mouth.

Chest

The chest (thorax) is a part of the anatomy of humans and various other animals located between the neck and the abdomen. It contains organs including the heart, lungs and thymus gland, as well as muscles and various other internal structures.

Chin

The area of the chin is known anatomically as the mental region. It tends to be smaller and more rounded in females, while bigger and more square in males. It is formed by the lower front of the mandible. In humans there is a wide variety of chin structures, e.g. cleft chin.

Ear

The ear is the organ that detects sound. It not only receives sound, but also aids in balance and body position. The ear is part of the auditory system. Often the entire organ is considered the ear, though it may also be considered just the visible portion.

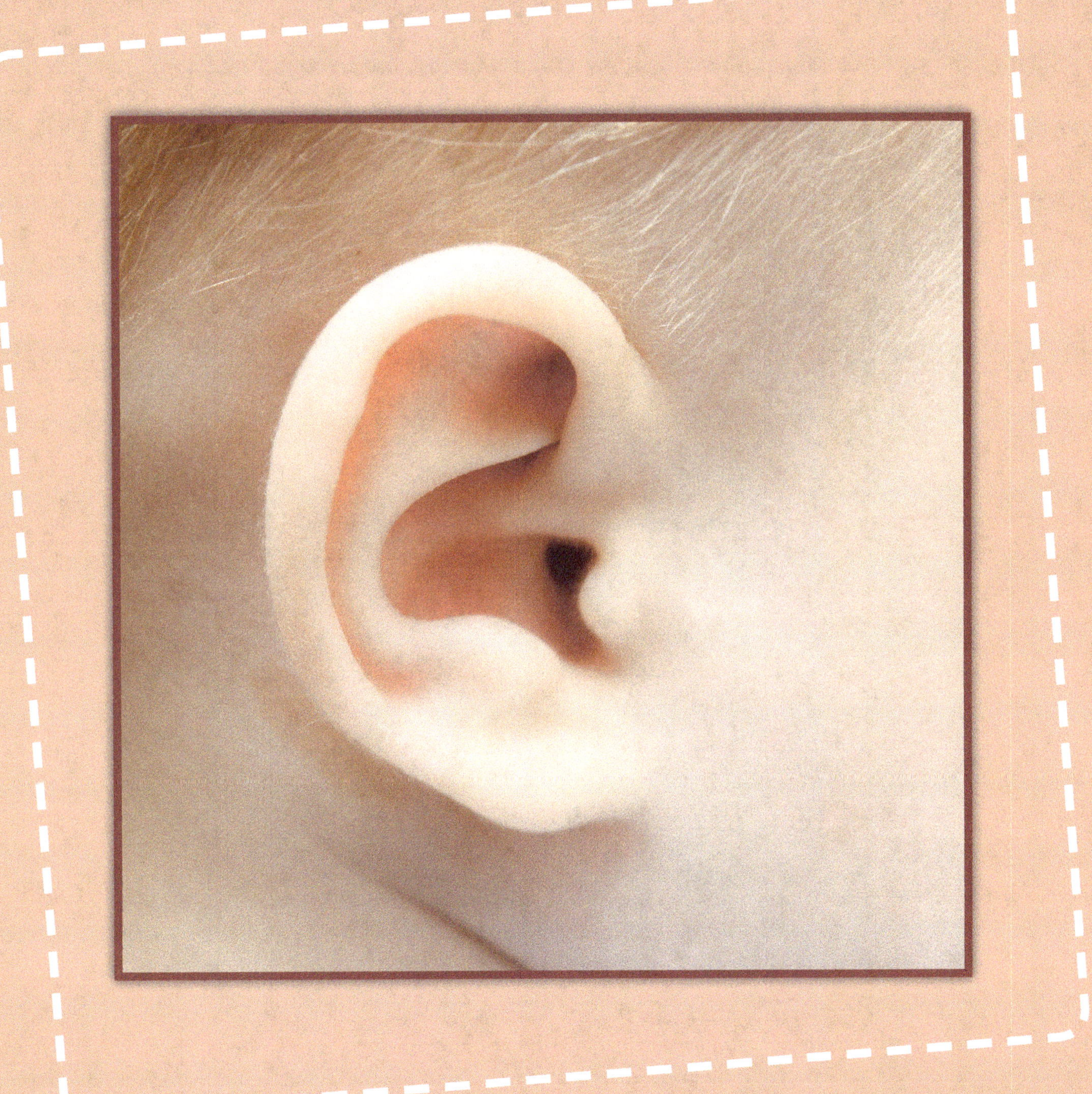

Eyebrow

The eyebrow is an area of thick, delicate hairs above our eyes. Their main function is hypothesized to prevent sweat, water, and other debris from falling down into the eye socket, but they are also important to human communication and facial expression.

Eyes

The human eye is an organ that reacts to light and has several purposes. Rod and cone cells in the retina allow conscious light perception and vision including color differentiation and the perception of depth. Our eyes can distinguish about 10 million colors.

Face

The face is a central organ of sense and is also very central in the expression of emotion among humans. The face is crucial for human identity, and damage such as scarring or developmental deformities have effects stretching beyond those of solely physical inconvenience.

Fingers

A finger is a limb of the human body found in our hands of humans. Normally humans have five fingers, the bones of which are termed phalanges, on each hand. The first digit is the thumb, followed by index finger, middle finger, ring finger, and little finger or pinky.

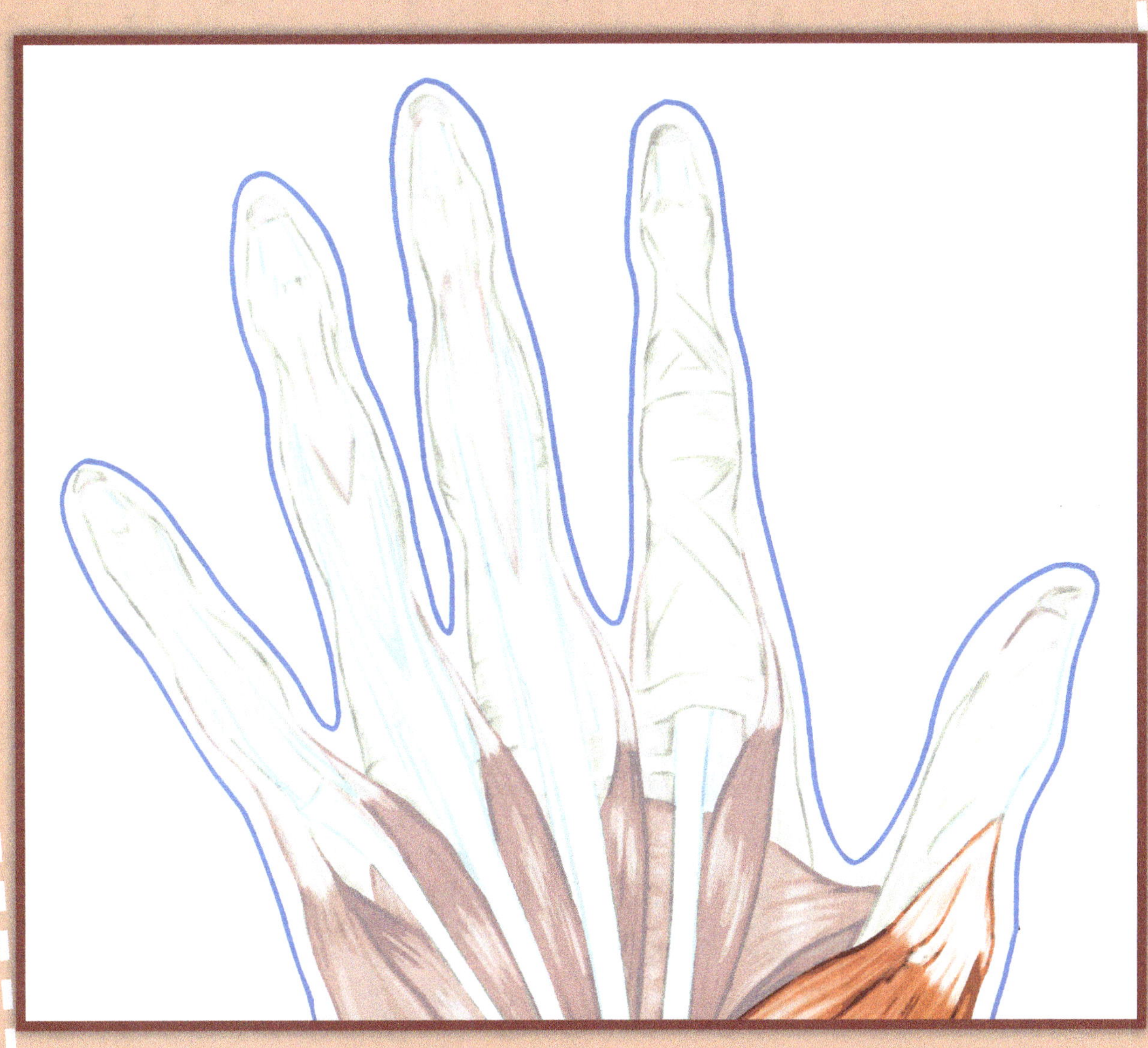

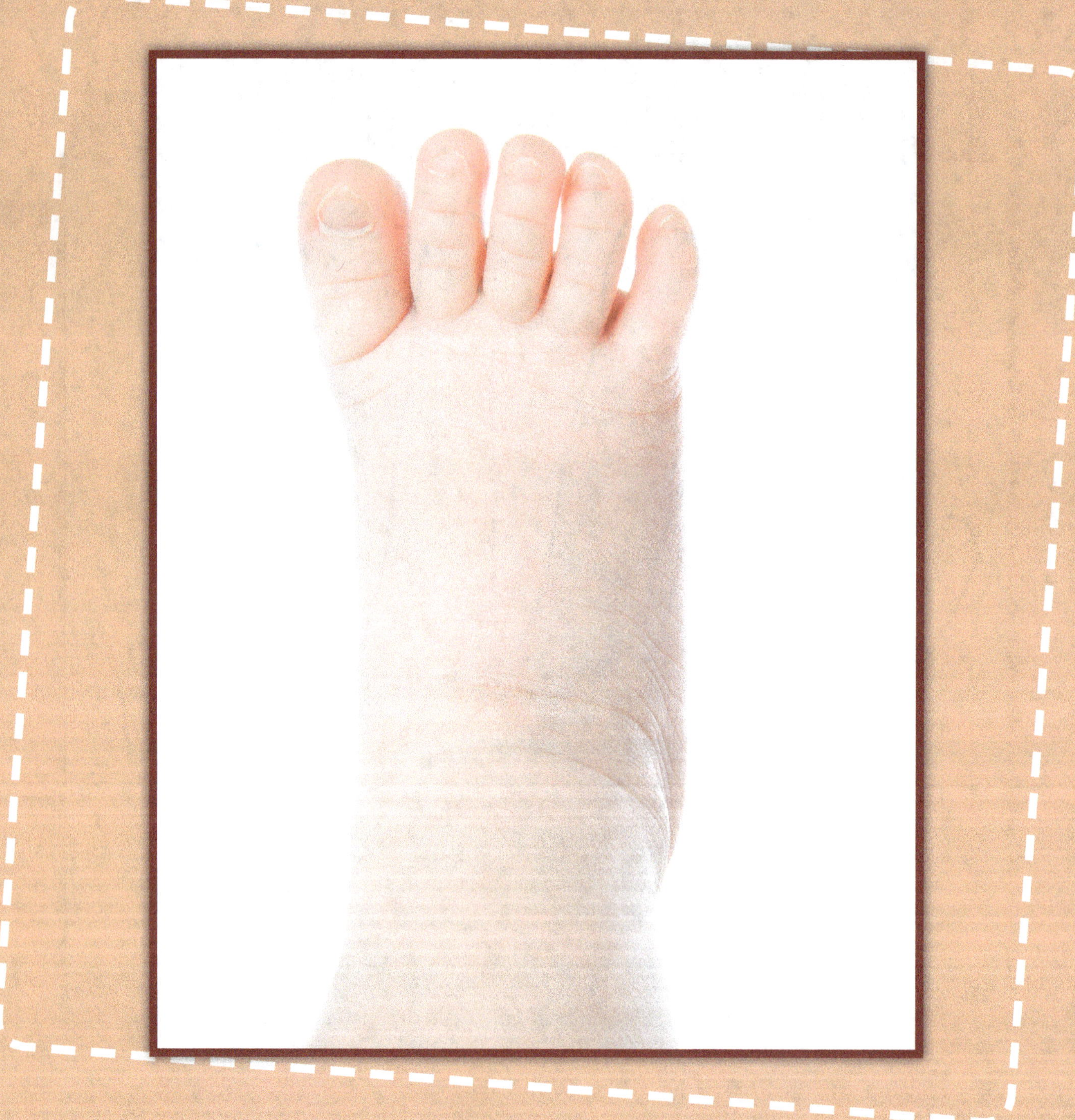

Foot

The foot is the terminal portion of a limb which bears weight and allows locomotion. In many animals with feet, the foot is a separate organ at the terminal part of the leg made up of one or more segments or bones, generally including claws or nails.

Forehead

The forehead is an area of the head bounded by three features, two of the skull and one of the scalp. The top of the forehead is marked by the hairline. The bottom of the forehead is marked by the bone feature of the skull above the eyes.

Hair

Hair is a protein filament that grows from follicles found in the skin. Most common interest in hair is focused on hair growth, hair types and hair care, but hair is also an important biomaterial primarily composed of protein, notably keratin.

Hand

The hand is a prehensile, multi-fingered extremity located at the end of an arm. The human hand is different to the hands of other animals, because it has fingers and a thumb that can work together.

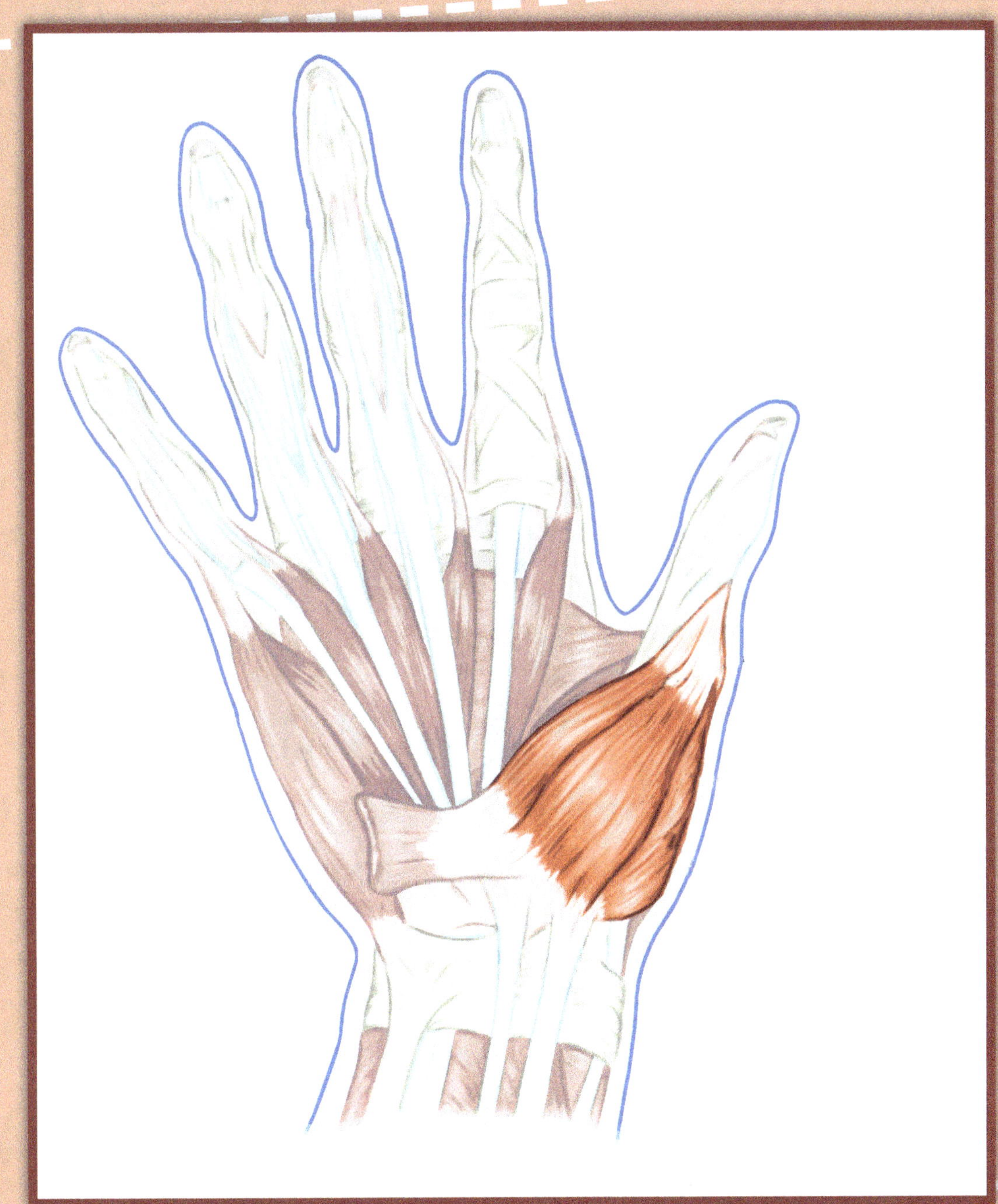

Knee

The knee joins the thigh with the leg and consists of two articulations: one between the femur and tibia, and one between the femur and patella. It is the largest joint in the human body. The knee joint is vulnerable to both acute injury and the development of osteoarthritis.

Leg

The human leg is the entire lower extremity or limb of the human body, including the foot, thigh and even the hip; however, the precise definition in human anatomy refers only to the section of the lower limb extending from the knee to the ankle.

Lip

Lips are a visible body part at the mouth. Lips are soft, movable, and serve as the opening for food intake and in the articulation of sound and speech.

Mouth

The mouth is the first portion of the alimentary canal that receives food and saliva. Human's mouth plays a significant role in communication. While primary aspects of the voice are produced in the throat, the tongue, lips, and jaw are also needed to produce the range of sounds included in human language.

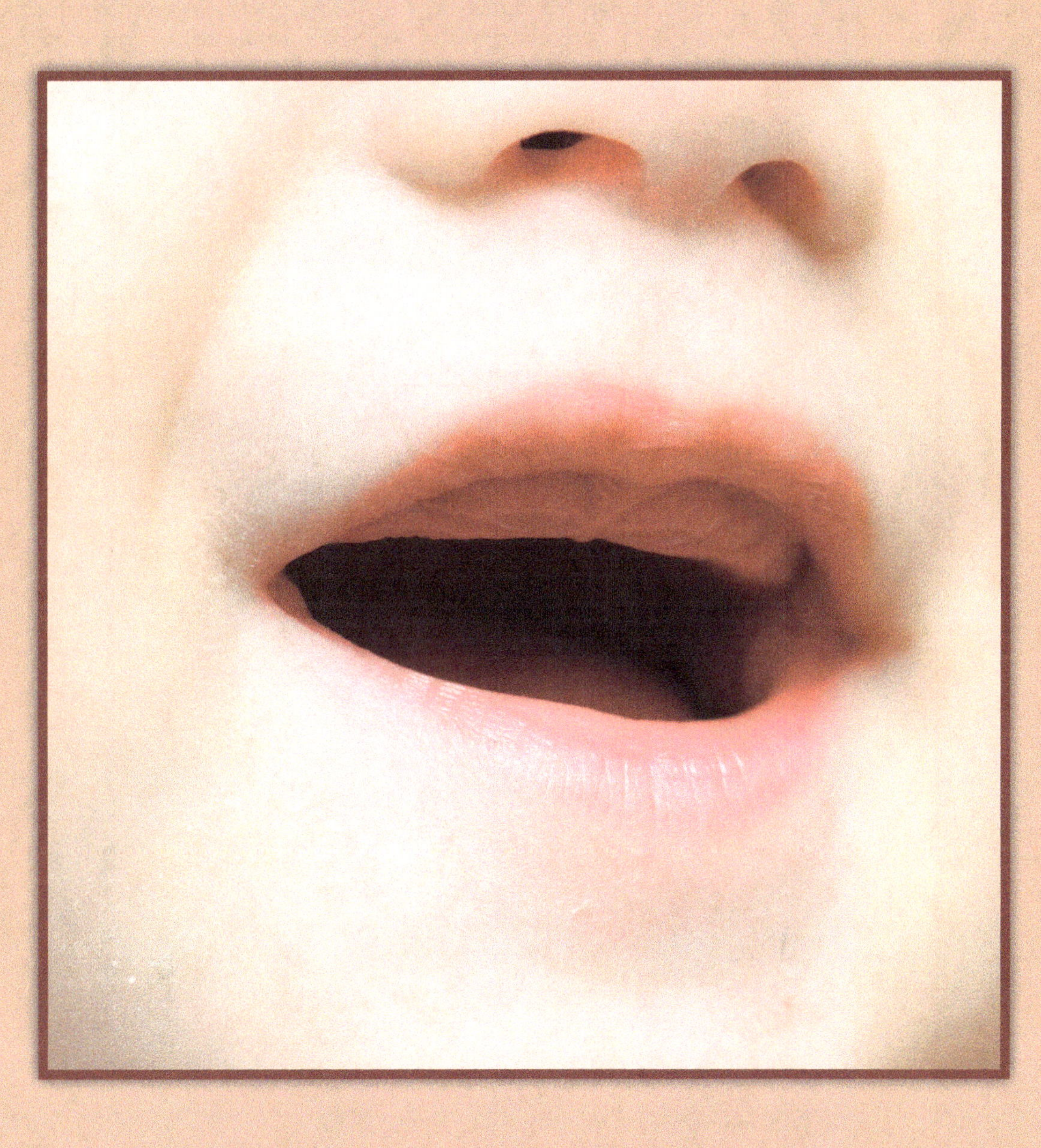

Nail

A nail is a horn-like envelope covering the tips of the fingers and toes in humans. Nails are similar to claws in other animals. Fingernails and toenails are made of a tough protective protein called keratin.

Neck

The neck is the part of the body that distinguishes the head from the torso or trunk. The human neck has the same number of vertebrae as giraffe's neck.

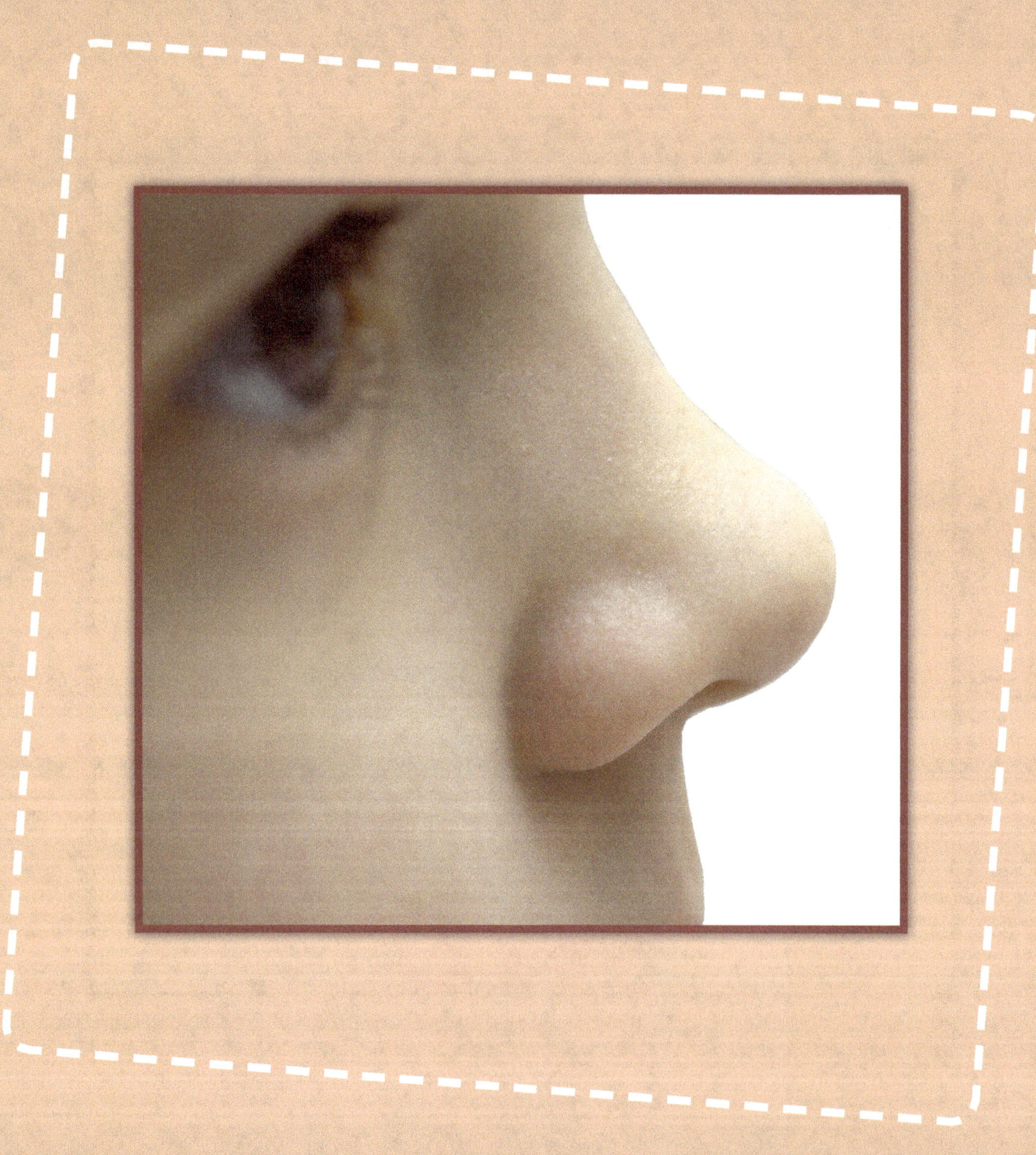

Nose

The visible part of the human nose is the protruding part of the face that bears the nostrils. The shape of the nose is determined by the ethmoid bone and the nasal septum, which consists mostly of cartilage and which separates the nostrils. On average the nose of a male is larger than that of a female.

Shoulders

The human shoulder is made up of three bones: the clavicle, the scapula, and the humerus as well as muscles, ligaments and tendons. The articulations between the bones of the shoulder make up the shoulder joints.

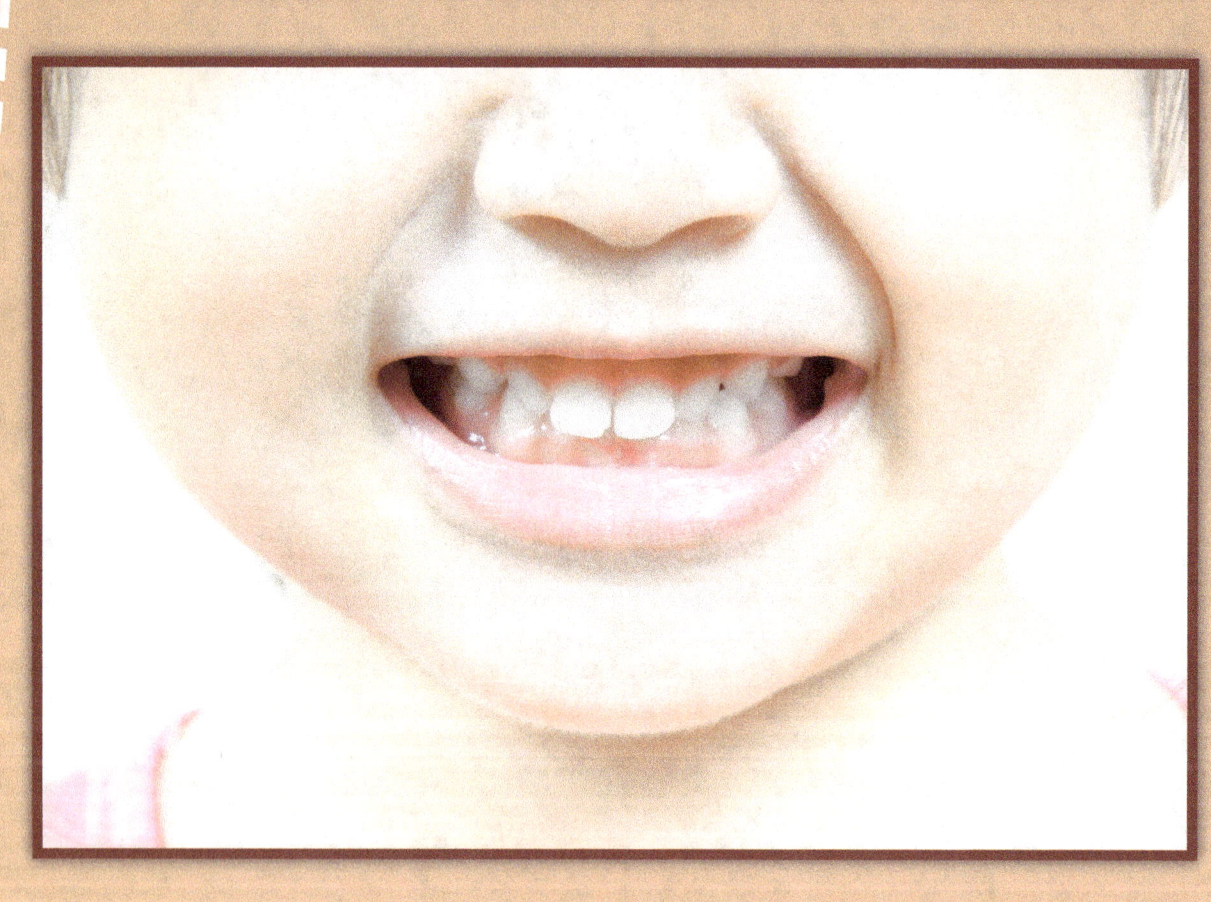

Teeth

Human teeth's function in mechanically breaking down items of food by cutting and crushing them in preparation for swallowing and digestion. The roots of teeth are embedded in the maxilla (upper jaw) or the mandible (lower jaw) and are covered by gums. Teeth are made of multiple tissues of varying density and hardness.